SOLILOQUY

What the soul says when no one's listening

DISHA SINGH

BookLeaf Publishing
India | USA | UK

Made with ❤ on the BookLeaf Publishing Platform
www.bookleafpub.in
www.bookleafpub.com

Dedication

To all those who write —

because the page listens when no one else does.

Preface

SOLILOQUYb is a conversation I've had with myself — in quiet hours, on restless nights, in moments too small to share but too heavy to hold. It's a collection of thoughts and feelings that surfaced when no one was watching, and no one was listening. There's no perfect order. No central theme. No attempt to follow rules or fit into a frame. Each poem comes from a different corner of me — some from joy, many from ache, and a few from places I still don't fully understand.

This isn't a book written to impress. It wasn't made to be liked or praised. It was made because I needed to write it. Because some feelings only make sense once they're out — spilled raw, without explanation, onto a page.

And maybe you're wondering —
if it was that personal, why share it at all?

Because I believe there's something quietly powerful in realizing you're not the only one who's felt a certain way. And if even one person finds a reflection in these pages — a line, a pause, a feeling — then sharing it was worth it.

This is me — unfiltered, unarranged, and maybe, a little more seen than I'm used to.

Thank you for listening to the part of me that usually stays quiet.

—Disha Singh

Acknowledgements

To my roots — my parents,
for giving me the ground to grow and the sky to reach.
To the ones who believed in me — Thank you.
Your quiet faith built more than you know.
You all helped me, even if you didn't realize it.

And to the voice that rose from within —
thank you for speaking,
even when everything else went silent.

And most importantly to Bookleaf Publishing,
for giving my words a place to truly exist.
Thank you for making this real.

Before the First Word

I sit, the pen, it shakes,
a question held in every break.
Should I write? Should I speak?
Or keep these secrets, still, so sleek?

The paper stares, it knows too well—
the lies I've lived, the stories I sell.
I try to hide, I try to mask,
but now the truth, it starts to ask—

Who are you? What will you show?
What's the cost of what you know?
It grips me tight, won't let me go.

I'm not sure I want to see,
the parts of me that aren't yet free.
The lies, the shame, the self-made chains,
the guilt, the fear, the endless pains.

Do I write the lie? Or face the truth?
What's more terrifying—words uncouth
or the silence that will steal my voice,
or the shame that leaves me no choice?

I feel it rise, deep in my chest—
the weight of all I've tried to suppress.
It swells, it twists, it begs to break,
to spill, to scream, to wake, to shake.

But still, I hesitate, I linger,
fingers trembling, no real figure,
just shadows circling, pulling tight,
a cage of doubt, a ghost of night.

What if I fail? What if I fall?
What if I'm nothing at all?
These thoughts scream louder, louder still,
and yet, they won't make my pen still.

A breath. A pause. A final look.
The mirror cracks. I take the hook.
I face it now, the raw, the real,
the wounds I've hid, the scars I feel.

The pen drops, I trust the flow,
I write it down, I let it go.
The truth is sharp, the truth is clear—
Before the First Word, I face the fear.

Beneath the Noise, There's Me

I don't run from quiet—
I rise in the still.
When the world goes loud,
I bend it to my will.

No crowd, no noise,
no need to prove—
I find my strength
in the silent groove.

Alone's not empty,
alone is mine.
It's sacred space,
it's self-defined.

They call it lonely—
I call it light.
It's where I train
when out of sight.

It's breath and beat,
it's calm, it's fire,
it's the echo deep

beneath desire.

No need for claps,
no stage, no show—
just me, my thoughts,
and how I grow.

So let them chase
the next big sound,
I build my throne
on quiet ground.

Solitude?
It's not a cage.
It's ink and fire,
it's war, it's page.

It's not my weakness.
It's my flame.
It's how I rise.
It's why I came.

The Mirror Doesn't Lie (But I Do)

The mirror shows me everything
I try to hide with careful light —
the cracks I fill with practiced smiles,
the tired eyes that beg for night.

I smooth my face, adjust my voice,
become the me they want to see.
But glass is cruel — it sees it all,
the ghost beneath who's still not free.

I lie in ways that sound like truth,
in laughter loud and eyes that shine.
I dress in strength, rehearse my lines,
then tell the world, "I'm doing fine."

But every night, when lights go low,
and silence sits across my skin —
the mirror waits, with patient breath,
to show me all I've held within.

It does not flinch. It does not speak.
It does not try to make me whole.

It only hands my image back
— and quietly reflects my soul.

Once Upon A Choice

Life is a story, a book of our own,
with pages unwritten, the future Unknown.

Each day a chapter, each choice a line,
A tale of wonder, uniquely mine.

Through highs & lows, through dark & light,
We hold the pen, we make it bright.

Mistakes are lessons, not the end,
A plot that bends, yet can transcend.

So dream with courage, write with grace,
Let hope & happiness fill every space.

For life's a story, fearless & free,
And the author? That is we.

I am A Woman

I am a woman, fierce and free,
in every breath, a symphony.
A force of nature, wild and untamed,
in every step, a dance unchained.

I am the fire that burns bright,
the spark that ignites the night.
With passion coursing through my veins,
I break the barriers, shatter chains.

I am the earth, grounded and wise,
nurturing life beneath azure skies.
With strength that flows from depths within
I rise above, I dare to win.

I am the water, fluid and pure,
flowing gracefully, ever sure.
In every ripple, a story untold,
in every wave, a spirit bold.

I am the air, swift and free,
whispering secrets through eternity.
With wings of dreams, I soar high,
embracing the vastness of the sky.

I am a woman, a force to be reckoned,
with dreams as vast as the heavens.
I am the embodiment of power ablaze,
a masterpiece of beauty and grace.

I am a woman, hear my roar,
I am the ocean, the sky, the core.
In every heartbeat, in every breath,
I am the essence of life and death.

So do not underestimate,
The strength that lies within my state.
For I am a woman, bold and true,
And there is nothing I cannot do.

Whispers Of Clouds

As I gazed upon the sky so grand,
the clouds whispered secrets,
like whispers from a band
"No more dwelling on regrets of days long past,
Time flies swiftly, Oh, it moves so fast,
Embrace the new commencement,
step out into the light,
let not emotions drown, cascading in the night

Within your heart, release memories to part,
For though it seems vast, it's a delicate art,
Hold firm to dreams, let them guide your way,
Take a respite, breathe, and let tears have their say,
For just as rain clears, revealing nature's art,
Happiness blooms, a fresh & vibrant start.

With each breakdown or pause, a rebirth is found,
A new beginning in life's symphony, profound,
So let the tears fall, like gentle drops of rain
And witness the joy that follows the pain
For after the same storm, a verdant world shall
surround,
A testament to healing, where happiness is found

Embrace the truth that unfolds with each refrain,
That after the rain, greenery & bliss shall remain.
let go of sorrow, free your spirit from its chain,
In the Symphony of life, a new chapter shall attain,
For every breakdown or pause a chance to ascend,
A journey towards happiness, a tale without end.

I Am Every Season

Spring does not arrive gently.
It breaks open the silence
with roots clawing through frozen ground –
as if to say,
growth is never soft.

The blossoms are not shy,
they bloom like a scream –
color returning to a soul
that forgot it was allowed to feel.

Summer scorches without apology.
It lays bare the bones of everything –
the roads crack, the air thickens,
and even the sky forgets how to breathe.

I am tired of pretending to shine.
This is not warmth.
This is a burning
that no one sees from afar.

Monsoon arrives like an apology too late –
loud, messy, impossible to ignore.
It pours where I never asked for healing,

and still I stand,
soaked in the weight
of everything I've never said aloud.

The sky cries first,
so I don't have to.
But I do anyway.

Autumn is where I begin to remember.
The trees shed like I wish I could –
guilt, fear, the expectations stitched into my skin.
They let go without asking for permission.
I only know how to hold.

The wind doesn't ask where I've been.
It just moves me.

Winter is the mirror.
There's no hiding in a season
that strips the world bare.
I watch myself disappear into white stillness,
and I don't fight it.
Some things must die
to be reborn honest.

And in the hush,
I hear it –

not the cold,
but the clarity.

Expectations Are Fatal

"Expectations are fatal," I said with a sigh,
As I watched another bright morning pass by.
They bloom in the chest like a well-meant lie,
Then vanish like smoke in a pale blue sky.

We dress up the future in ribbons and lace,
Give names to the shadows we're longing to face.
But nothing arrives quite the way that we dream—
It's never that simple, it's never that clean.

Expectations are fatal, like sugar in wine,
They sweeten the edge of a bitter design.
You sip and you hope, but it always goes cold—
The warmth that you wanted replaced by the mold.

We wait for a word, for a look, for a sign,
We script out the scenes in the back of our mind.
But people aren't stories, and life doesn't read
The lines we rehearsed in our moment of need.

Expectations are fatal—so leave them behind,
Let moments arrive without shapes you've defined.
What is will become, with or without your say,
And peace sometimes lives in just being okay.

Possibilities Are Numerous

I think too much, I always do –
A thought begins, then splits in two.
And two birth four, and four birth ten,
I live a thousand lives – and then...

A look, a word, a moment small,
Becomes a story I recall.
Though it was never said or done,
I've lived it all – and everyone.

I plan the fall before I climb,
Rewrite the past a hundred times.
I speak aloud in empty air,
To ghosts of people never there.

I dream of things I'll never face,
Then panic in an untouched space.
What if I fail? What if they go?
What if they see I'm just a show?

I want to rest, to press "rewind,"
Escape the corners of my mind.
But possibilities don't cease –
They fight my thoughts, they steal my peace.

So here I sit, a worn-out maze,
Inside a mind that never stays.
And still I say, with practiced grace,
"I'm fine" — while lost in every place.

Anatomy of the Void

I was born into a question
no one remembers asking.
A name assigned, a path suggested—
but never a why carved into the marrow.

The mirror shows a shape that breathes,
but not a self I recognize.
Flesh moves, routines repeat,
yet something in me remains uninhabited.

What is this life,
if not a sequence of masks layered over silence?
Purpose feels like a myth
told to soothe the ache of waking.

I search in books, in voices,
in the tremble between sleep and waking—
but answers dissolve like fog,
always just out of reach.

Do I want meaning, or do I want escape?
Is longing a flaw, or the only proof
that I am real?

I fear that all of this—
the joy, the pain, the wanting—
might be motion without memory,
a flicker in a system that doesn’t care.

But still, I ask.
Still, I ache.
Still, I breathe.

Not because I understand—
but because I don't.
Because silence hasn't answered me,
and maybe it won't.

And if this is all there is—
just echoes in a hollow shell—
then let them be mine.
Let me be the scream
that no one needed to hear
but still existed.

The One Who's Always Okay

I say "I'm fine"
so often
my tongue forgets how to say anything else.
It rolls off easy,
like a reflex.
Like breathing.
Like lying.

I laugh at the right time,
ask the right questions,
hold space for every storm that isn't mine.
And when the room empties –
so do I.

I am tired
of answering messages I wish I never got.
Tired of carrying grief
with hands that no one holds.
Tired of being the lighthouse
when all I want is
to be found.

I shrink in crowds.

I nod through noise.
I play the part.
And still,
no one notices the silence beneath my yes.

Some nights, I don’t even cry –
not because it doesn't hurt,
but because even sadness
feels like effort.

I’m tired of pretending
this body is not breaking.
Tired of being the one who understands
while no one asks
if I’m okay.

I don’t know what kind of tired this is –
only that it lives
in my bones,
my breath,
my name.

I Remember Wrong

I twist the truth, I make it bend,
I shape the past, I fake the end.
The moments fade, the edges blur,
I force my heart to make a cure.

I told myself I'd let it go,
But memories creep, they start to show.
I tell myself, "No, it's not real,"
But it lingers still, it makes me feel.

I bury the pain, I hide the trace,
I paint a smile to hide the space.
I tell myself, "It's all erased,"
But something here can't be replaced.

I remember wrong,
But I force the lie.
I tell my heart,
"Don't ask why."

In the quiet dark,
I twist the truth,
But in the back of my mind,
I hear the proof.

I shut my eyes,
I turn the page,
I try to burn
the past's old cage.

But it comes again,
It won't let go,
The memories tug,
They start to show.

I try to erase,
I try to forget,
But the echoes ring,
And I regret.

I remember wrong,
But I can't deceive,
No matter how hard
I try to leave.

The Storm Isn't Over

The skies went blue, the winds grew still,
But something shakes me deeper still.
They say, "It's passed," with calm belief,
Yet I still tremble underneath.

The rain has stopped – the ground is dry,
But thunder echoes when I cry.
They see the sun and call it peace,
But I still beg for the release.

No shattered trees or shattered glass,
No proof that something came to pass.
But inside me, the winds still wail,
And every breath feels frail, feels pale.

I smile to make the silence stay,
But lightning sparks in things I say.
I flinch at calm, at touch, at sound –
There's war within, though none around.

They ask me why I can't move on,
Why fear still sings when pain is gone.
But healing's not a tidy feat –
The storm still lives beneath my feet.

It hides in dreams, in quiet nights,
In harmless words that turn to fights.
It twists my peace, it steals my air –
The world looks fine. But it's still there.

So don't mistake my steady gaze,
For calm that came in healing's phase.
The sky may clear, the winds may slow –
But the storm in me...
won't let me go.

The Room with No Windows

I live in a room with no windows or light,
Where morning is endless and day becomes night.
The walls do not echo, the air doesn't sing,
And silence itself feels like tightening string.

The door is not locked – there's no key, no chain,
Yet somehow I'm stuck in the shape of my pain.
No shadows to chase, just a dull, aching grey,
Where even my thoughts have begun to decay.

The ceiling is low, like a weight on my chest,
The corners are lined with the dreams I suppressed.
I speak, but my voice doesn't carry or bend –
It dies in the air with no one to defend.

I've tried to escape with a smile or two,
But plaster can crack and expose what is true.
They ask me to "try" – and I nod like I should,
But trying feels harder than being understood.

There's no clock that ticks, no sound of the rain,
Just echoes of memories wrapped up in pain.
I am not asleep, but I don't feel awake –

This room is a cage that no one can break.

Still, deep in the corner, a flicker remains,
A whisper of colour resisting the chains.
And maybe one day, when I gather the will,
This room will have windows –
and sunlight, will spill.

Solace By the Sea

The sea gives me solace, its depth so profound,
as I sit beside the shore, lost in thoughts, I am bound.
I ponder the question, with a mind so astute.
How can the busy sea give me solace so absolute?

Beneath the sky's canvas, vast and wide,
The waves in their rhythm, a timeless tide.
They speak in whispers, both ancient and deep,
A philosophical puzzle in their secrets to keep.

The world may rush by with its chaos and haste,
Yet the sea stays steadfast in its tranquil embrace.
In its constant motion, a lesson I find,
That solace can dwell in the busiest of times.

For the sea, like life, knows both storm & calm,
It's waves can be gentle, or raise a loud psalm.
In its ebb & its flow, a reflection I see,
of the cycles we all face, in our own journey.

So, as I sit by the shore, with the sea as my guide,
I learn from its wisdom, in its rythmic stride.
The busy world may chum, with its endless demand,
But the sea gives me solace, in its ever-present hand.

In the eons it is witnessed, in the stories untold,
The sea holds the secrets, of both young & old.
It teaches me patience in a world that's in a hurry,
That true solace, like the sea, is a timeless deep journey...

In Shadows' Embrace

Who am I? lost in shadows' gloom,
a waning moon or just a stain to loom?
With every breath, does pain persist,
peace eludes, a sorrow's clenching fist.

Am I a flame, once fierce and bright,
now ashes cold, devoid of light?
Or merely a drop, lost in the sea,
drowning in waves of uncertainty?

Within myself, I seek the key,
to unlock the truth, set my soul free.
Yet, with question left unmet,
I wander further, lost and upset.

In shadows' embrace, I find no peace,
As doubts and fears refuse release.
Amidst the darkness, a soul confined,
yearning for answers i cannot find.

I Am So Done

I am so done with this chaos called life,
A never-ending loop of struggle and strife.
Wake up, survive, repeat, pretend—
When does this nonsense ever end?

Dreams dissolve like smoke in the air,
Promises broken, no one to care.
Every damn step is a stumble, a fall,
I scream for help, but there's no one to call.

The clock ticks on, a cruel, dull joke,
Hope is a fire that's smothered in smoke.
Tired of trying, tired of pain,
Tired of losing again and again.

But even as I curse and sigh,
Somehow, still, I don't say goodbye.
Maybe tomorrow will bring something new—
Or maybe I'm just a fool, it's true.

Beneath the Veil Of Sorrow

In shadows deep, I wander lost,
Seeking solace at any cost.
Each moment a struggle, each day a trial,
In this weary world, I bear no smile.

Every step I take, burdened & weighed,
By the darkness that within me is laid.
A prisoner to sorrow, I strive to breakfree,
To craft a realm where my soul can see.

In the echoes of silence, my heart does plea,
for a glimmer of hope to set me free.
Yet the darkness persists, ten relentless & Stark
As I navigate through this desolate park.

But still I dream of a brighter day,
Where my own world I shall array.
Though the path is fraught & the journey long,
I'll persist, for in hope, I find my song.

So, I will weave my tale, with threads of pain,
And in the midst of despair, I'll find my gain.
For in the depths of sorrow, I'll carve my way,
To a realm of my own, Where I'll finally stay.

Flawed Fragility

In fields of Expectation, I bloom,
A flower of Perfection, in endless rooms.
Each petal poised, each stem erect,
I dance to the tune of what's correct.

But burdened by the weight of flawless grace,
I fear the fall from my revered place.
My soul, a bird with clipped wings,
In cages of expectation, it sings.

Why must I be a flawless stone,
When nature's beauty in flaws is shown?
The rose that blooms with thorns so sharp,
Yet in its imperfection, captures the heart.

Like a tree, I yearn to sway bend & sway,
Not always standing tall, come what may.
For in the forest of life's trials and tests,
Its the broken branches that nature bestows its best.

So let me embrace the storm's fierce gale,
And let my flaws become my tale.
For in the wilderness of self-acceptance, I'll find,
The beauty of being imperfectly divine.

Labyrinth Of Choices

In a Realm of Choices vast, a traveler lost,
Paths converge, decisions at great cost.
A maze of options, each a tempting call,
Yet uncertainty looms, shadows fall.

Amidst the crossroads, whispers of fate,
A symphony of choices, an intricate debate.
Which path to tread, in this tangled array?
Each step a gamble, a role to play.

In the labyrinth of life, profound maze,
Every route adorned with a different haze.
The weight of decisions, a burden to bear,
Every path chosen, a challenge to dare.

Battles await at each turn taken,
A relentless cycle, a destiny shaken.
Yet courage rises, a flame within,
To face the struggles, to strive & win.

The journey unfalds with twists untold,
A tapestry of stories, of silver & gold.
In every direction, a tale to weave,
The lost soul strives, determined to acheive.

Through the chaos, a compass found,
Guided by dreams, on solid ground.
For in the heart of the maze, a truth to glean,
The path chosen shapes the destiny seen.

The Sky Is Not My Limit

In dreams of daring, I aspire to soar,
to grasp the unattainable, to seek much more.
Beyond the crowd's embrace, I'll find my space,
A shade apart, where uniqueness finds it grace.

A whisper in the wind, a blaze of light,
I'll chase the stars that gleam in the night.
Limitless horizons, I aim to explore,
for the sky is not my limit,I'll reach for more.

With courage as my guide, I'll break the chains,
unraveling possibilities, embracing gains.
No limits hold me back, no boundaries confine,
I'll paint my destiny across the cosmic design.

So let them call me bold,unconventional, and rare,
I'll carve my legacy beyond compare.
For in the realm of dreams, I'll take my flight,
acheiving the unacheivable with all my might.